When We Reach the Edge,

Where Do We Go for Support?

BRENDA A. JENKINS

*Priority*ONE
p u b l i c a t i o n s
Detroit, MI USA

When We Reach the Edge, Where Do We Go for Support?
Copyright © 2003 Brenda A. Jenkins.

Reprinted from HELP! for Your Leadership, Chapter 7.
Used by Permission

All scripture quotations, unless otherwise indicated, are taken from the HOLY BIBLE, NEW INTERNATIONAL VERSION®. NIV®. Copyright ©1973, 1978, 1984 by International Bible Society. Used by permission of Zondervan. All rights reserved.

Scripture quotations marked (AMP) are taken from the Amplified Bible, Copyright © 1954, 1958, 1962, 1964, 1965, 1987 by The Lockman Foundation. Used by permission.

Out of reverence and honor for God's Word, the word Bible is capitalized throughout this work. Also throughout this work the name of satan is not capitalized in order to re-emphasize Christ's victory over him.

All rights reserved. No part of this publication may be reproduced, stored in a retrieval system, or transmitted in any form or by any means – electronic, mechanical, photocopy, recording, or any other – except for brief quotations in printed reviews, without the prior permission of the publisher.

*Priority*ONE Publications
P. O. Box 725 • Farmington, MI 48332
(800) 331-8841 Nationwide Toll Free
(313) 893-3359 Southeast Michigan
E-mail: info@p1pubs.com
URL: http://www.p1pubs.com

ISBN: 0-9703634-4-3

Cover and interior design by *PriorityONE Publications*
Printed in the United States of America

Table of Contents

1. Introduction 1
2. Possible Signs That You Need Help 2
3. Self Assessment......................................7
4. Time with God 14
5. Mentors..16
6. Core Groups 17
7. Professional Counselor 18
8. Support Groups 20
9. Church 21
10. Biblical Counseling.............................22
11. Steps for Improvement 23
12. Summary...24
References 26
About Brenda A. Jenkins...........................27

Introduction

Your success and happiness lie in you...
Resolve to keep happy, and your joy and you
shall form an invincible host against difficulties.
-- Helen Keller

People helpers are always helping others. In this journey of helping others, we can get to a point of burnout. How do you draw the line between helping others and helping yourself? Does that die to self, really mean, kill your "self" physically? No, it means letting Jesus be Lord in your life. Let your steps be ordered by the Lord.

"If the Lord delights in a man's way, he makes his steps firm; though he stumble, he will not fall, for the Lord upholds him with his hand" (Psalm 37:23-24).

Many times we don't recognize we are giving too much of ourselves until we are at the point of falling. For the high achievers, survivors, and overcomers who feel they have many people depending on them, anxiety sets in and they get to a point of being ineffective in their work. We could be doing the responsibilities of others. Because these people's work is above average, no one notices the problems or they may think no one notices. Who do you go to? Who would understand?

The objectives of this chapter are:(1) to help you recognize your need for help (2) and to give some suggested courses of action to become more victorious in your life.

According to Romans 14:17, *"the Kingdom of God is... righteousness, peace and joy in the Holy Spirit."* As you read through this chapter, try to focus on getting yourself better for God's work. You will be presented with many methods, pick one or use them all. Yes, there is a call on your life. We have to be in shape to execute God's call. I will use the Bible, reference materials I have read, and my personal experiences to share so that you too can attain help as you continue on this journey on earth.

Possible signs that you are in need of help

The problem: many times leaders get off the path, they don't realize God has changed their call, they may be overworked, not taking time for rest and fellowship, don't have boundaries in their life, or just forgot that in the beginning God did great things in six days. The seventh day He rested. Jesus rested many times. Not enough rest is only one problem. I am sure you can name many other reasons leaders get to the point that they need help. It is important that leaders recognize they have a problem. Let's look at some other signs. You can check off the ones that apply to you.

_____ You go home to sleep; rarely do you eat there or enjoy your castle.

_____ Your neighbors only see you a couple of times in each season.

_____ Your every waking hour is occupied with tasks to complete.

_____ Your family has to make an appointment to get to see you or talk with you.

_____ You send emails in the middle of the night.

_____ You have piles of paperwork all over your house including your bed.

_____ Only the high priority tasks are taken care of.

_____ Tasks on the "to do" list stay there until they get to a high priority status.

_____ 24 hours is not enough in a day you would like 36.

_____ You grab a nap wherever you can (car, restroom, doctor's office, etc.).

_____ You are multi-tasking.

_____ You do not have time for the mishaps that life presents.

_____ Most teams want you on their team (known for getting the job done).

© 2003 Brenda A. Jenkins

Don't misunderstand the list. This leader is also making things happen. Their ministry is growing and they probably can do every job in the ministry. Their life was not always like this. They are the ones who see a dream and make it come true, even if they have to do it all by themselves. You are in ministry; you make things happen but at the expense of you and your family. Everyone comes to you with his or her problems. You are the leader right?

When I looked up the word overworked, the definitions were an eye opener. Work too hard or too long. Work that is too severe or burdensome. Work beyond the amount agreed upon. The synonyms were just as eye opening. Too busy, overburdened, worked too hard; see

tired. I went to the word tired. Fatigue, worn-out or weary. It states "*SYN.*--**tired** is applied to one who has been drained of much of his strength and energy through exertion, boredom, impatience, etc. *[tired* by years of hard toil*]*; **weary** (or **wearied**) suggests such depletion of energy or interest as to make one unable or unwilling to continue *[weary* of study*]*; **exhausted** implies a total draining of strength and energy, as after a long, hard climb; **fatigued** refers to one who has lost so much energy through prolonged exertion that rest and sleep are essential *[fatigued* at the end of the day*]*." (Compton's Interactive Encyclopedia © 1999 The Learning Company, Inc.) Can you relate to one or more of the above? If so, read on.

Now for some of us, we may mistake the word tired with tried. Tested, trustworthy, faithful, having endured trials and troubles are what is described as being tried.

Synonyms for tried are dependable, proved, approved, certified and used. I may have stepped on many toes, and the question becomes, how do I know if I am tired, or I am being tried?

The theme of Psalm 1 is that life has two roads. The balanced life of the faithful person is contrasted with the faithless person. What is the motive behind what you do? Is it self-satisfaction or to the glory of God?

The totality of life includes work, school (whatever you do for self-improvement), rest, exercise, relationships (with God and people), personal finances, family, and church.

Overachievers and workaholics, like other addictions, call for a total restructuring of one's life. Many times when you produce good results, people, including yourself, don't see the addictive behavior.

We have requirements that must be meet in life to make us complete. Do we know what the requirement of life is? Using God's standards, how do you measure up?

Before we do this assessment, write your vision statement for life. God's word says, *"Where there is no vision, the people will perish"* (Proverb 29:18 KJV). Your vision looks beyond where you are today. Once you have written your vision, write your mission statement. (This is how you plan to carry out the vision.)

Now that you have your vision and mission written, let's look at some of the requirements of life. I have included a few assessment charts after the following questions. The questions, lists, and charts are just a sample of the responsibilities in some areas in life. They are not inclusive and are presented to start a process within you of what your responsibilities may be in life.

Self Assessment

1. **Scripture tells us to: seek the kingdom God and His righteousness first. (Matthew 6:33)**

    Are you building your intimate relationship with God? You ask, "How do I know?" Are you worshipping God, doing Bible study, witnessing, praying, and providing service? Do you love God with all your heart, soul, and mind? (Matthew 22:37)

ASSESSMENT #1 - Kingdom Building

Matthew 6:33	Measurable Results		
	Daily	Weekly	Monthly
Worshipping God Spending time with God			
Bible Study			
Witness to others about the kingdom			
Praying			
Providing Service			

Checks in shaded area are to be added to your development plan

2. How are your social relationships?

Healthy relationships are important. Do you allow time for fellowship? Many who are having relationship problems with others don't really trust God and may not have that intimate relationship with Him. Before doing your assessment, I would like to make sure we are using the same definition of social relationship.

Social is "of or having to do with human beings living together as a group in a situation in which their dealings with one another affect their common welfare." (Compton's Interactive Encyclopedia © 1999 The Learning Company, Inc.) To be social is getting along well with others.

For our purpose, let's define others as friends, members of a group, co-workers, neighbors, and church members. To build healthy relationships, it requires time, sharing, honesty, love, boundaries, and intercessory prayer. *"How good and pleasant it is when brothers live together in unity." (Psalm 133:1)*

3. **Knowing, developing, and using your gifts (talents).**

Are you being the best that you can be? God has given all of us at least one gift.

"Each one should use whatever gift he has received to serve others, faithfully administering God's grace in its various forms." (1 Peter 4:10)

Do you know what your gift(s) are? Are you using it to God's glory? In 1 Corinthians 12:7-10, the manifestation gifts are listed. These gifts are the supernatural manifestations of the Holy Spirit at work through the believer. In Ephesians 4:11-16, Paul lists the ministry gifts used for maturing the saints. Also, in Romans 12:6-8, Paul mentions the seven motivational gifts. Whatever your gift, it must be used with God's agape love. For more information on spiritual gifts see the book by Don & Katie Fortune entitled, *Discover Your God-Given Gifts*. Look at the two charts below on spiritual gifts. If you know your gift, what stage of operation are you in (identifying, developing, or operating)?

ASSESSMENT #2
Ministry Spiritual Gifts: For the building up of the body of Christ (What is yours?)

Ephesians 4:11-16	Measurable Results		
	Identified	Developing	Operating In
Apostle function			
Prophet function			
Evangelist function			
Pastor function			
Teacher function			

Checks in shaded area are to be added to your development plan.

ASSESSMENT #3
Motivational Gifts: Gifts to benefit one another
(What is yours?)

Romans 12:6-8	Measurable Results		
	Identified	Developing	Operating In
Perceiver	▓	▓	
Server	▓	▓	
Teacher	▓	▓	
Exhorter	▓	▓	
Giver	▓	▓	
Administrator	▓	▓	
Compassion	▓	▓	

Checks in shaded area are to be added to your development plan

4. Single/Married Life has its own set of responsibilities.

ASSESSMENT #4

Single	Married	
	Husband	Wife
Must stay sexually pure 1 Corinthians 6:9-10, 7:7-9 Maintain a special relationship with God – 1 Corinthians 7:32 God's business is their business	Loving leaders Ephesians 5:25 Love your wife, and be not bitter against them – Colossians 3:19 Support family, sexual pleasure 1 Corinthians 7:1-5; Proverbs 5:18-19	Must show respect, take care of home, and be helpmate Proverbs 31, Ephesians 5:22-33, 1 Corinthians 11:3. Submit to own husband, as it is fit to the Lord Colossians 3:18

5. **Parenting (Proverbs 22:6):**
   _____ raise up a child to know and love God (Deuteronomy 6:4 – 9)
   _____ provide love (1 Corinthians 13)
   _____ provide instruction (11 Timothy 3:14 – 17, Proverb 1:8, Proverb 6:20)
   _____ loving discipline (Proverbs 29:17, Proverbs 19:18, Proverbs 29:15)
   _____ fathers do not provoke (Ephesians 6:4, Colossians 3:21)

6. **Good steward of finances:**
   _____ Do you have a budget? (Luke 14:28)
   _____ Goal is to be debt free (Romans 13:8)
   _____ First fruits go to God, tithes & offerings (Malachi 3:8-12, Proverbs 3:9-10)

7. **Health – eating right and exercise.**
   It is so vital that you take care of your physical body – eating healthy meals, exercise, getting regular doctor and dentist check-ups.

   After completing your assessment, you may be able to determine areas for improvement. Write out a development plan. Work your plan.

Time with God

God knows everything about us. How do you spend time with God? First and foremost, you must take a break with God. This is time for you and God. This means away from home, work, ministry, family, and friends. Everything must be put on hold. A friendly warning, you can initiate the time out, or God will. It is your choice.

In my Christian walk, I have learned that it is important to take responsibility for what happens in your life, and be accountable for your actions. You did not just happen to be at this place. You made some choices to get yourself here. God is faithful; he is always with us.

"No temptation has seized you except what is common to man. And God is faithful; he will not let you be tempted beyond what you can bear. But when you are tempted, he will also provide a way out so that you can stand up under it." (1 Corinthians 10:13)

When you get in God's presence, God's holiness, then you can clearly see your sin and you must confess.

"For my thoughts are not your thoughts, neither are your ways my ways, declares the Lord. As the heavens are higher than the earth, so are my ways

higher than your ways and my thoughts than your thoughts." (Isaiah 55:8-9)

God cleansed Isaiah and gave him His plan. Isaiah had to get in God's presence, in His holiness. It was at this point that Isaiah knew he was unclean before God with no hope of measuring up to God's standards. When his lips were touched with burning coal, God forgave his sins. Isaiah accepted his call from God but not before he allowed God to purify him. He submitted to God's will for his life.

Before we can represent God, we must allow Him to purify us. This can be a painful process, but it is necessary to represent God. After this process, God asked, "Whom shall I send?" Isaiah said, "Here am I, send me."

According to the *Life Application Bible*, page 1161, Isaiah is considered the greatest prophets of the Old Testament. He had to deliver the message, judgment, and hope to people who had little positive response. (Isaiah 6: 1-13)

One of the questions I mentioned earlier in this chapter was what is the difference between tired and tried? You become tired when you are working in your own strength, past your limits. Tried is when you have God's peace and you allow Him to control your life while going through the trials. Learn how to get in His presence and hear from Him.

Mentors

A mentor may be called a coach, guide, or teacher. All of us are teachers at some time in our life. Good teachers are learners first.

"I delight in learning so that I can teach." – Seneca

"Those having torches will pass them on to others." – Plato

"Who dares to teach must never cease to learn." – John Cotton Dana (apples & chalkdust by Vicki Caruana)

Grandkids are an opportunity to do mentoring in your family. This is an investment into the future. There are two words that I teach all of my grandchildren, responsibility and accountability. It is really fun being a grandparent. You give and receive so much love.

You are not the primary caregiver. I hope you are able to get your grandkids when you want, and then send them back home. As the grandkids grow, teach them that they are role models/mentors for the younger grandkids. God created a repeatable process.

Core Group

A core group or peer group is a group of equals in something. This could be age, status, work, ministry, etc. Within this group, each of the people can relate to each other. They accept each other just the way they are. They confront each other for the betterment of each other. They support each other, and they trust each other.

Everyone does not fit into this group. The people in this group may change as life's circumstances change. You select people to fit into this group. This group is generally very small (two or three). Trust and loving confrontation are important to the success of the core group. When mistakes are made, it is vital that each person repents of their sin and asks forgiveness. We do not want to store up resentment and bitterness. If this step is not done, it will affect the effectiveness of the group. You have to love each other enough to go through the pain that may come from confrontation.

Are you a trusting person? You may want to complete the trust assessment chart in chapter 3 (HELP! for Your Leadership) and add any improvements needed to your development plan.

When you confront others, you must remember to edify the person (Ephesians 4:29). Accept people for who they are, don't try to make them like you or you try to be like them.

Rebecca Florence Osaigbovo's, book entitled, *Movin' On Up,* does an excellence job of describing moving beyond religion to spirit living. She describes the four levels of walking in the spirit ankle deep, knee deep, loin deep, and rivers. We have to continue developing our spiritual walk. Rebecca states, *"We won't move on up to Spirit living, if we don't risk being transparent with other members of our spiritual family."* (Osaigbovo, 1984, p. 163)

If the members of the group do not grow and do not receive and give loving confrontation to each other, you no longer have an effective core group.

Professional Counseling

There may come a time when you need someone that you do not have available in any of your support groups. You may be overextended and don't want to burden others with all you are going through. When you are experiencing pain and have much to deal with, you may need one-on-one attention. Someone who would be unbiased and knowledgeable of the area in which you are having problems, who listens to you so they can hear what the problem is, and most importantly, someone you can trust.

All of us fall short of perfection and have hidden pains no one knows about but God. Many times people don't understand that God provides help in many forms. There are some issues God provides gifted people to help. Professional Counselors' skills are gifts from God. If there are wounds that have not been exposed, they can creep out and create problems in other areas of your life.

Professional counselors can help sort through the issues that are within. Don't let pride and shame keep you from getting mentally healthy. Like with other support person(s), you need a common value system. It is important that as a consumer, you must take care in choosing a professional counselor/therapist. Check out their credentials first and make sure that you check with people who are familiar with their work.

In the book, *Safe People,* it is stated, *"There are many good people out there. To find them, make sure that you use discernment, wisdom, and information, and trust your experience with people. If someone is destructive or producing bad fruit in your life, be careful. Keep looking, praying, and seeking until you find safe people-people who will give you all the benefits that God has planned for you."* (Cloud, Townsend, 1995, p. 168)

Sometimes you may have a problem that those close to you really don't see as a problem from their frame of reference. If they don't see the problem, then it is impossible for them to advise you properly, or you could be in denial and not really telling everything because you really don't know what the problem is. Seeing a trained professional counselor who is unattached and listens tentatively could make all the difference in correcting the problem.

"For lack of guidance a nation falls, but many advisers make victory sure." (Proverbs 11:14)

Support Group

A support group is a group of people working on similar goals. Their express purpose is to help hurting people. Some examples are: twelve step programs, prayer groups, therapy groups, single parents, sexual abuse survivors, etc.

It is important that you have experienced leadership in these groups. These groups can be very powerful. *The Help Book* (United Way Tel-Help Information and Referral Services), lists many support groups with reference numbers. It also lists other agencies that are available to help people in resolving problems. To get the help you need check these groups. Don't let one bad experience prevent you from trying another. Confidentiality and trust are important. You have to be willing to work on yourself.

Church

Join a Bible teaching church. The church is another support system. The pastor is gifted to deliver the word of God for everyday life applications. He/she also will hold you accountable for walking the Christian walk. The church is like a hospital; many are sick, looking for help. Make sure the church has many ministries that address the needs you are looking for. If you like the church and a particular ministry is not there, talk with your pastor about starting one. Know that anywhere people are, there will be the issues of life.

We are all sinners. Know your God given goal, work your plan, and trust God. *"And we know that in all things God works for the good of those who love him, who have been called according to his purpose" (Romans 8:28).*

Biblical Counseling

This is a ministry generally under the umbrella of a church. The pastor is the overseer. Laymen and women are trained to apply the Bible to their every day life. As they grow spiritually, they start counseling others using the Bible. Their opinions have no place in the counseling sessions, the Word of God is the only authority used. Confidentiality is critical. The lay counselor must live their lives, using the skills they have learned, and share God's Word. *"Brothers, if someone is caught in a sin, you who are spiritual should restore him gently. But watch yourself, or you also may be tempted. Carry each other's burdens, and in this way you will fulfill the law of Christ." (Galatians 6:1-2)*

ASSESSMENT #5 – Available Support

Support	Yes	No
God		
Mentors		
Core Groups		

Professional Counseling		
Biblical Counseling		
Church		
Support Groups		

Choose the ones that are best suited for your situation

Steps for Improvement

1. Know what your call is and write your vision and mission statement.
2. Do an assessment in all the areas of your life. See assessment charts in this booklet and chapter 3 of HELP! for Your Leadership.
3. Based on your assessment, write a development plan.
4. Work your plan.
5. Do periodic check ups to make sure you are on track.
6. Repeat the process. This may be done more often when you have multiple issues. Take one day at a time, one issue at a time.

Summary

Sometimes we get too busy being busy, that we don't hear from God. Take some time away, fast, and pray. Ask for forgiveness for getting yourself in such a rut. Ask for wisdom from God to show you what it is He wants you to do.

I took a day away from my busy life to talk with God and discovered He wanted me to write and speak. He wanted me to start doing more intercessory prayer. So being the organized person that I am, I starting writing down all that I was doing.

It is so very important to be obedient to God, loving and trusting Him to take care of the desires of your heart. Once you realize that no matter what is going on around you, if you stay focused on God, doing His will, you will have peace and joy. Think about Peter. He walked on water as long as he kept his focus on God.

I have shared some of my experiences, problem-solving skills, and used numerous Scriptures in hope that it will help someone else. You need to know what your call is from God. You need to do an assessment of your life to see if you are on target for that call. When God calls you, He will also equip you. You also need to know when you need help (we are not a island and definitely not Jesus Christ, only He saves.) We need God and we need people.

Oh Heavenly Father,
I am so thankful for You. I love being in Your presence. I praise You. Your hand keeps me lifted even when I do not have the strength to lift myself. Lord, I thank You for providing me with so many people to love. Lord, teach me and search my heart. Heal me, Lord. If You decide not to heal, lead me to be satisfied anyway. I am learning, Lord, that joy is my love for You and my trust in You that You will take care of my household and me. Please forgive me of my sins and teach me to forgive others as You have forgiven me. In Jesus' Name – Amen.

References

1. Barbas, Stacey and Manning, Lyn *The Help Book*. Tel-Help, United Way Community Services, 1999.

2. Caruana, Vicki 2002. *the complete apples & chalkdust*. P.O. Box 55388, Tulsa, Oklahoma, 74155, RiverOak Publishing.

3. Cloud, Henry and Townsend, John, D 1995. *Safe People*. Grand Rapids, Michigan 49530, Zondervan.

4. Fortune, Don and Fortune, Katie 1996. *Discover Your God-Given Gifts*. P.O. Box 6287, Grand Rapids, Michigan 49516-6287, Chosen Books a division of Baker Book House Company, Eighteenth printing, December.

5. Osaigbovo, Rebecca Florence 1997. *Movin' On Up "A Woman's Guide Beyond Religion to Spirit Living* P.O. Box 35377, Detroit Michigan, 48235, Dabar Publishing Co.

6. *The Compton's Interactive Encyclopedia* 1999. The Learning Company, INC.

7. Tyndale House Publishers. *Life Application Bible King James Version*. Wheaton, Illinois, Tyndale House Publishing, Inc.

About Brenda A. Jenkins

Brenda loves people. She states her purpose is to take her gifts and skills to help others. She is very transparent and has no problem sharing her victories overcoming rough times in her life. Brenda has the ability to see the expected outcome of any task and works to put plans in place to reach that end.

Brenda is well-versed in problem-solving, organizational and interpersonal skills. The Foundation for all that she does rests in her strong commitment to the Word of God. She is the mother to four adult children and the proud grandmother to twelve grandchildren.

At New Hope Missionary Baptist Church in Southfield, Michigan, Brenda served faithfully for seven years as the Ministry Director of the Biblical Counseling Ministry; a ministry birthed under her leadership. Currently, she is the Counseling Advisor and Outreach Facilitator for this ministry. As a Certified Biblical Counselor and adjunct instructor for Christian Research and Development, she teaches classes that will build up students and prepare them to confront themselves and counsel others with the Bible as the guidebook.

As CEO of ARIEL Connections her passion is "Providing Relationship Solutions to Organizations that Value People."

For more information or to book Ms. Jenkins for speaking engagements, or radio and television interviews contact:

ARIEL Connections
P.O. Box 22, Royal Oak, MI 48068-0022
email: brenda.jenkins@ameritech.net
website: ariel-connections.com
Phone: (313) 719-1621

A - Accept
R - Relate
I - Invest
E - Encourage
L - Love

Leaving the
Lone Ranger Mentality – Alone!

Name _____
Address _____
City _____ State _____ Zip _____
Phone _____ Fax _____
Email _____

Quantity	
Price *(each)*	$4.99
Subtotal	
S & H *(each)*	$0.99
MI Tax 6%	
TOTAL	

METHOD OF PAYMENT:
❑ Check or Money Order
(*Make payable to*: **PriorityONE Publications**)
❑ Visa   ❑ Master Card   ❑ American Express
Acct No. _____
Expiration Date (*mmyy*) _____
Signature _____

Mail your payment with this form to:
PriorityONE Publications
P. O. Box 725, Farmington, MI 48332
(800) 331-8841 – Toll Free
(313) 893-3359 – Southeast Michigan
URL: http://www.p1pubs.com
Email: info@p1pubs.com

When We Reach the Edge, Where Do We Go for Support?

Name _____
Address _____
City _____ State _____ Zip_____
Phone _____ Fax _____
Email _____

Quantity	
Price *(each)*	$4.99
Subtotal	
S & H *(each)*	$0.99
MI Tax 6%	
TOTAL	

METHOD OF PAYMENT:
❏ Check or Money Order
(*Make payable to*: **PriorityONE Publications**)
❏ Visa ❏ Master Card ❏ American Express
Acct No. _____
Expiration Date (*mmyy*) _____
Signature _____

Mail your payment with this form to:
PriorityONE Publications
P. O. Box 725, Farmington, MI 48332
(800) 331-8841 – Toll Free
(313) 893-3359 – Southeast Michigan
URL: http://www.p1pubs.com
Email: info@p1pubs.com

HELP! For Your Leadership

Name _____
Address _____
City _____ State _____ Zip_____
Phone _____ Fax _____
Email _____

Quantity	
Price *(each)*	$14.99
Subtotal	
S & H *(each)*	$2.99
MI Tax 6%	
TOTAL	

METHOD OF PAYMENT:
❏ Check or Money Order
(*Make payable to*: **PriorityONE Publications**)
❏ Visa   ❏ Master Card   ❏ American Express
Acct No. _____
Expiration Date (mmyyyy) _____
Signature _____

Mail your payment with this form to:
PriorityONE Publications
P. O. Box 725, Farmington, MI 48332
(800) 331-8841 – Toll Free
(313) 893-3359 – Southeast Michigan
URL: http://www.p1pubs.com
Email: info@p1pubs.com

Be on the lookout for these future books by
Brenda A. Jenkins

(2005) Black, Sabrina D, Dixon, Christina, Hudson, Pamela J, Jenkins, Brenda A. *HELP! For Your Leadership Leaders Self Care Workbook.* Detroit, Michigan; PriorityONE Publications

(2005). *ARIEL Connections Relationship Model: Building Relationships that Last.* Detroit, Michigan; PriorityONE Publications

(2006). *"Out of Your Pain: "You Are Who You Are".* (TNT) Detroit, Michigan; PriorityONE Publications

(2006). *"HELP! for Parents".* (TNT) Detroit, Michigan; PriorityONE Publications